Milemarkers

A 5 Year Journey

This journal belongs to:

MILEMARKERS: A 5 Year Journey

Cover design by Deanne Vick

Edited by Stacy Davis

Printed in the United States of America

First Edition 2019

ISBN-13: 978-0578496948

www.brucewaller.com

MILEMARKERS: A 5 Year Journey

In 1998, my wife purchased a journal as a gift for me to write down my thoughts during my grandmothers last days. It started the journey of writing, reflecting, and sharing with others. I later received some of my grandmother's journals from my mom and experienced great joy reading her thoughts and sayings she lived by each day.

Capturing our stories is just as important today. Each time we write something down, it becomes a Milemarker in life and helps us reflect on past, present, and future. *Milemarkers: A 5-Year Journey* was developed as a tool to help you record an amazing collection of your special moments so that you may share with others. When we share what's inside our heart, it allows us to reflect on our blessings and fills us with gratitude to experience joy in our life. This journal will one day be a treasure for the one that holds it next!

Here are 10 ideas to help capture your Milemarkers journey:

1. Share gratitude daily.
2. Write down children or grandchildren sayings.
3. Share moments you experience in the workplace.
4. Capture family events.
5. Track health and wellness activity.
6. Write down things you learn each day.
7. Write down favorite Bible readings.
8. Use it to note important tasks to complete.
9. Track personal goals or professional development.
10. Write down anything that brings you joy each day.

Daily journaling allows you to reflect on moments from the previous year, and month-end questions will help make your 5-year journey complete.

The important thing is to develop the habit of writing each day. Write with purpose. It will absolutely change your life.

Find your lane and track milemarkers to capture your amazing journey. Share on social media with #milemarkers and let's experience our journey together.

Wishing you success!

Bruce W. Waller

JANUARY 1

20_____

_____
_____
_____
_____

20_____

_____
_____
_____
_____

20_____

_____
_____
_____
_____

20_____

_____
_____
_____
_____

20_____

_____
_____
_____
_____

"There are 86,400 seconds in the day. It's up to you to decide what to do with them." Jim Valvano

JANUARY 2

20_____

_____
_____
_____
_____

20_____

_____
_____
_____
_____

20_____

_____
_____
_____
_____

20_____

_____
_____
_____
_____

20_____

_____
_____
_____
_____

JANUARY 3

20_____

_____

_____

_____

_____

20_____

_____

_____

_____

_____

20_____

_____

_____

_____

_____

20_____

_____

_____

_____

_____

20_____

_____

_____

_____

_____

"The purpose of life is to live with Purpose."
Anonymous

JANUARY 4

20_____

_____
_____
_____
_____

20_____

_____
_____
_____
_____

20_____

_____
_____
_____
_____

20_____

_____
_____
_____
_____

20_____

_____
_____
_____
_____

JANUARY 5

20_____

_____

_____

_____

_____

20_____

_____

_____

_____

_____

20_____

_____

_____

_____

_____

20_____

_____

_____

_____

_____

20_____

_____

_____

_____

_____

"Be yourself because everybody else is already taken."
Oscar Wilde

JANUARY 6

20_____

_____
_____
_____
_____

20_____

_____
_____
_____
_____

20_____

_____
_____
_____
_____

20_____

_____
_____
_____
_____

20_____

_____
_____
_____
_____

JANUARY 7

20_____

_____

_____

_____

_____

20_____

_____

_____

_____

_____

20_____

_____

_____

_____

_____

20_____

_____

_____

_____

_____

20_____

_____

_____

_____

_____

"Learn to move past the distractions and you will succeed." Jesse Itzler

JANUARY 8

20____

_____
_____
_____
_____

20____

_____
_____
_____
_____

20____

_____
_____
_____
_____

20____

_____
_____
_____
_____

20____

_____
_____
_____
_____

MILEMARKERS

JANUARY 9

20_____

_____

_____

_____

_____

20_____

_____

_____

_____

_____

20_____

_____

_____

_____

_____

20_____

_____

_____

_____

_____

20_____

_____

_____

_____

_____

"It takes a long time to be an overnight success!"
Simon Sinek

JANUARY 10

20_____

_____
_____
_____
_____

20_____

_____
_____
_____
_____

20_____

_____
_____
_____
_____

20_____

_____
_____
_____
_____

20_____

_____
_____
_____
_____

MILEMARKERS

JANUARY 11

20_____

_____

_____

_____

_____

20_____

_____

_____

_____

_____

20_____

_____

_____

_____

_____

20_____

_____

_____

_____

_____

20_____

_____

_____

_____

_____

"To be influential we must be open to influence."
Brendon Burchard

JANUARY 12

20_____

_____
_____
_____
_____

20_____

_____
_____
_____
_____

20_____

_____
_____
_____
_____

20_____

_____
_____
_____
_____

20_____

_____
_____
_____
_____

JANUARY 13

20_____

_____
_____
_____
_____

20_____

_____
_____
_____
_____

20_____

_____
_____
_____
_____

20_____

_____
_____
_____
_____

20_____

_____
_____
_____
_____

"Selling is not telling." Charlie Bell

JANUARY 14

20_____

_____

_____

_____

_____

20_____

_____

_____

_____

_____

20_____

_____

_____

_____

_____

20_____

_____

_____

_____

_____

20_____

_____

_____

_____

_____

JANUARY 15

20_____

_____

_____

_____

_____

20_____

_____

_____

_____

_____

20_____

_____

_____

_____

_____

20_____

_____

_____

_____

_____

20_____

_____

_____

_____

_____

"These are moments that define who you become."
Stephanie Waller

JANUARY 16

20_____

_____
_____
_____
_____

20_____

_____
_____
_____
_____

20_____

_____
_____
_____
_____

20_____

_____
_____
_____
_____

20_____

_____
_____
_____
_____

MILEMARKERS

JANUARY 17

20_____

_____
_____
_____
_____

20_____

_____
_____
_____
_____

20_____

_____
_____
_____
_____

20_____

_____
_____
_____
_____

20_____

_____
_____
_____
_____

"We cannot always build the future for our youth, but we can build our youth for the future." Franklin Roosevelt

JANUARY 18

20_____

_____
_____
_____
_____

20_____

_____
_____
_____
_____

20_____

_____
_____
_____
_____

20_____

_____
_____
_____
_____

20_____

_____
_____
_____
_____

JANUARY 19

20_____

_____
_____
_____
_____

20_____

_____
_____
_____
_____

20_____

_____
_____
_____
_____

20_____

_____
_____
_____
_____

20_____

_____
_____
_____
_____

"Leaders must set the expectations." Heitor Defaria

JANUARY 20

20_____

_____
_____
_____
_____

20_____

_____
_____
_____
_____

20_____

_____
_____
_____
_____

20_____

_____
_____
_____
_____

20_____

_____
_____
_____
_____

MILEMARKERS

JANUARY 21

20_____

_____
_____
_____
_____

20_____

_____
_____
_____
_____

20_____

_____
_____
_____
_____

20_____

_____
_____
_____
_____

20_____

_____
_____
_____
_____

"A watched pot never boils." Ancient Proverb

JANUARY 22

20____

_____
_____
_____
_____

20____

_____
_____
_____
_____

20____

_____
_____
_____
_____

20____

_____
_____
_____
_____

20____

_____
_____
_____
_____

MILEMARKERS

JANUARY 23

20_____

_____

_____

_____

_____

20_____

_____

_____

_____

_____

20_____

_____

_____

_____

_____

20_____

_____

_____

_____

_____

20_____

_____

_____

_____

_____

"Whenever you see a successful business, someone once made a courageous decision." Peter Drucker

JANUARY 24

20_____

_____
_____
_____
_____

20_____

_____
_____
_____
_____

20_____

_____
_____
_____
_____

20_____

_____
_____
_____
_____

20_____

_____
_____
_____
_____

JANUARY 25

20_____

_____
_____
_____
_____

20_____

_____
_____
_____
_____

20_____

_____
_____
_____
_____

20_____

_____
_____
_____
_____

20_____

_____
_____
_____
_____

"Freedom lies in being bold." Robert Frost

JANUARY 26

20_____

_____
_____
_____
_____

20_____

_____
_____
_____
_____

20_____

_____
_____
_____
_____

20_____

_____
_____
_____
_____

20_____

_____
_____
_____
_____

JANUARY 27

20_____

_____
_____
_____
_____

20_____

_____
_____
_____
_____

20_____

_____
_____
_____
_____

20_____

_____
_____
_____
_____

20_____

_____
_____
_____
_____

"When the student is ready, the teacher will appear."
Ancient Proverb

JANUARY 28

20_____

_____

_____

_____

_____

20_____

_____

_____

_____

_____

20_____

_____

_____

_____

_____

20_____

_____

_____

_____

_____

20_____

_____

_____

_____

_____

JANUARY 29

20_____

_____

_____

_____

_____

20_____

_____

_____

_____

_____

20_____

_____

_____

_____

_____

20_____

_____

_____

_____

_____

20_____

_____

_____

_____

_____

"Happiness is when what you think, what you say, and what you do are in harmony." Mahatma Gandhi

JANUARY 30

20_____

_____
_____
_____
_____

20_____

_____
_____
_____
_____

20_____

_____
_____
_____

20_____

_____
_____
_____
_____

20_____

_____
_____
_____
_____

MILEMARKERS

JANUARY 31

20_____

_____

_____

_____

_____

20_____

_____

_____

_____

_____

20_____

_____

_____

_____

_____

20_____

_____

_____

_____

_____

20_____

_____

_____

_____

_____

"Your level of success will never exceed your level of personal development." Jim Rohn

Monthly Reflections...

Where was I born?

_____

_____

_____

_____

Where did I grow up?

_____

_____

_____

_____

What was my first job?

_____

_____

_____

_____

"We can issue you everything, but desire!"
Coach Walter Causey

FEBRUARY 1

20_____

_____
_____
_____
_____

20_____

_____
_____
_____
_____

20_____

_____
_____
_____
_____

20_____

_____
_____
_____
_____

20_____

_____
_____
_____
_____

_"When our values are clear, our choices are easier
in all areas of our life."_ Bruce Waller

FEBRUARY 2

20_____

_____
_____
_____
_____

20_____

_____
_____
_____
_____

20_____

_____
_____
_____
_____

20_____

_____
_____
_____
_____

20_____

_____
_____
_____
_____

FEBRUARY 3

20_____

_____
_____
_____
_____

20_____

_____
_____
_____
_____

20_____

_____
_____
_____
_____

20_____

_____
_____
_____
_____

20_____

_____
_____
_____
_____

"A devotion to serving others is one of the most important values in a man." George H. W. Bush

FEBRUARY 4

20_____

_____
_____
_____
_____

20_____

_____
_____
_____
_____

20_____

_____
_____
_____
_____

20_____

_____
_____
_____
_____

20_____

_____
_____
_____
_____

FEBRUARY 5

20_____

_____

_____

_____

_____

20_____

_____

_____

_____

_____

20_____

_____

_____

_____

_____

20_____

_____

_____

_____

_____

20_____

_____

_____

_____

_____

"Be the best YOU that YOU can be." Ozzie Smith

FEBRUARY 6

20_____

_____

_____

_____

_____

20_____

_____

_____

_____

_____

20_____

_____

_____

_____

_____

20_____

_____

_____

_____

_____

20_____

_____

_____

_____

_____

FEBRUARY 7

20____

_____
_____
_____
_____

20____

_____
_____
_____
_____

20____

_____
_____
_____
_____

20____

_____
_____
_____
_____

20____

_____
_____
_____
_____

_"If you are going to be a champion, you must be willing
to pay a greater price."_ Bud Wilkinson

FEBRUARY 8

20_____

_____
_____
_____
_____

20_____

_____
_____
_____
_____

20_____

_____
_____
_____
_____

20_____

_____
_____
_____
_____

20_____

_____
_____
_____
_____

MILEMARKERS

FEBRUARY 9

20_____

_____
_____
_____
_____

20_____

_____
_____
_____
_____

20_____

_____
_____
_____
_____

20_____

_____
_____
_____
_____

20_____

_____
_____
_____
_____

"If you look for the bad in people expecting to find it, you surely will." Abraham Lincoln

FEBRUARY 10

20_____

_____
_____
_____
_____

20_____

_____
_____
_____
_____

20_____

_____
_____
_____
_____

20_____

_____
_____
_____
_____

20_____

_____
_____
_____
_____

MILEMARKERS

FEBRUARY 11

20_____

_____
_____
_____
_____

20_____

_____
_____
_____
_____

20_____

_____
_____
_____
_____

20_____

_____
_____
_____
_____

20_____

_____
_____
_____
_____

"We must find time to stop and thank the people who make a difference in our lives." John F. Kennedy

FEBRUARY 12

20_____

_____
_____
_____
_____

20_____

_____
_____
_____
_____

20_____

_____
_____
_____
_____

20_____

_____
_____
_____
_____

20_____

_____
_____
_____
_____

MILEMARKERS

FEBRUARY 13

20_____

_____
_____
_____
_____

20_____

_____
_____
_____
_____

20_____

_____
_____
_____
_____

20_____

_____
_____
_____
_____

20_____

_____
_____
_____
_____

"Your actions are so loud I can't hear you."
Ralph Waldo Emerson

FEBRUARY 14

20_____

_____
_____
_____
_____

20_____

_____
_____
_____
_____

20_____

_____
_____
_____
_____

20_____

_____
_____
_____
_____

20_____

_____
_____
_____
_____

MILEMARKERS

FEBRUARY 15

20_____

_____

_____

_____

_____

20_____

_____

_____

_____

_____

20_____

_____

_____

_____

_____

20_____

_____

_____

_____

_____

20_____

_____

_____

_____

_____

"In matters of style, swim with the current. In matters of principle, stand like a rock." Thomas Jefferson

FEBRUARY 16

20_____

_____
_____
_____
_____

20_____

_____
_____
_____
_____

20_____

_____
_____
_____
_____

20_____

_____
_____
_____
_____

20_____

_____
_____
_____
_____

MILEMARKERS

FEBRUARY 17

20_____

_____
_____
_____
_____

20_____

_____
_____
_____
_____

20_____

_____
_____
_____
_____

20_____

_____
_____
_____
_____

20_____

_____
_____
_____
_____

"All a man needs is a pocket knife and a pencil."
Dewey Ivey

FEBRUARY 18

20_____

_____
_____
_____
_____

20_____

_____
_____
_____
_____

20_____

_____
_____
_____
_____

20_____

_____
_____
_____
_____

20_____

_____
_____
_____
_____

FEBRUARY 19

20_____

_____
_____
_____
_____

20_____

_____
_____
_____
_____

20_____

_____
_____
_____
_____

20_____

_____
_____
_____
_____

20_____

_____
_____
_____
_____

"Never miss a chance to ask a question and learn something new." Paige Lueckemeyer

FEBRUARY 20

20_____

_____
_____
_____
_____

20_____

_____
_____
_____
_____

20_____

_____
_____
_____
_____

20_____

_____
_____
_____
_____

20_____

_____
_____
_____
_____

MILEMARKERS

FEBRUARY 21

20_____

_____
_____
_____
_____

20_____

_____
_____
_____
_____

20_____

_____
_____
_____
_____

20_____

_____
_____
_____
_____

20_____

_____
_____
_____
_____

"There is no limit to the amount of good you can do if you don't care who gets the credit." Ronald Reagan

FEBRUARY 22

20_____

_____
_____
_____
_____

20_____

_____
_____
_____
_____

20_____

_____
_____
_____
_____

20_____

_____
_____
_____
_____

20_____

_____
_____
_____
_____

MILEMARKERS

FEBRUARY 23

20_____

_____

_____

_____

_____

20_____

_____

_____

_____

_____

20_____

_____

_____

_____

_____

20_____

_____

_____

_____

_____

20_____

_____

_____

_____

_____

"What you get by achieving your goals is not as important as what you become by achieving your goals." Zig Ziglar

FEBRUARY 24

20_____

_____

_____

_____

20_____

_____

_____

_____

_____

20_____

_____

_____

_____

20_____

_____

_____

_____

_____

20_____

_____

_____

_____

_____

MILEMARKERS

FEBRUARY 25

20_____

_____

_____

_____

_____

20_____

_____

_____

_____

_____

20_____

_____

_____

_____

_____

20_____

_____

_____

_____

_____

20_____

_____

_____

_____

_____

"A bad attitude is like a flat tire, you can't go anywhere until you change it!" Anonymous

FEBRUARY 26

20_____

_____

_____

_____

_____

20_____

_____

_____

_____

_____

20_____

_____

_____

_____

_____

20_____

_____

_____

_____

_____

20_____

_____

_____

_____

_____

MILEMARKERS

FEBRUARY 27

20_____

_____
_____
_____
_____

20_____

_____
_____
_____
_____

20_____

_____
_____
_____
_____

20_____

_____
_____
_____
_____

20_____

_____
_____
_____
_____

"Culture is what you permit and promote."
Charlyn Renfrow

FEBRUARY 28

20_____

_____
_____
_____
_____

20_____

_____
_____
_____
_____

20_____

_____
_____
_____
_____

20_____

_____
_____
_____
_____

20_____

_____
_____
_____
_____

MILEMARKERS

FEBRUARY 29

20____

_____
_____
_____
_____

20____

_____
_____
_____
_____

20____

_____
_____
_____
_____

20____

_____
_____
_____
_____

20____

_____
_____
_____
_____

"My goal is to be a better man today than I was yesterday." Charles Haley

Monthly Reflections...

How did I get started in my career?

_____

_____

_____

_____

My first car:

_____

_____

Life lesson(s) I learned growing up:

_____

_____

_____

_____

_____

_____

"If you could get all the people in an organization rowing in the same direction, you could dominate any industry, in any market, against any competition, at any time." Patrick Lencioni

MARCH 1

20_____

_____

_____

_____

_____

20_____

_____

_____

_____

_____

20_____

_____

_____

_____

_____

20_____

_____

_____

_____

_____

20_____

_____

_____

_____

_____

"Success will not always bring you happiness, but happiness will always bring you success." Albert Schweitzer

MARCH 2

20_____

_____
_____
_____
_____

20_____

_____
_____
_____
_____

20_____

_____
_____
_____
_____

20_____

_____
_____
_____
_____

20_____

_____
_____
_____
_____

MARCH 3

20_____

_____
_____
_____
_____

20_____

_____
_____
_____
_____

20_____

_____
_____
_____
_____

20_____

_____
_____
_____
_____

20_____

_____
_____
_____
_____

"The doors will be opened to those who are bold enough to knock." Tony Gaskins

MARCH 4

20_____

_____
_____
_____
_____

20_____

_____
_____
_____
_____

20_____

_____
_____
_____

20_____

_____
_____
_____
_____

20_____

_____
_____
_____
_____

MILEMARKERS

MARCH 5

20_____

_____
_____
_____
_____

20_____

_____
_____
_____
_____

20_____

_____
_____
_____
_____

20_____

_____
_____
_____
_____

20_____

_____
_____
_____
_____

"The bigger your DREAM, the more important your TEAM." Darren Hardy

MARCH 6

20____

_____
_____
_____
_____

20____

_____
_____
_____
_____

20____

_____
_____
_____
_____

20____

_____
_____
_____
_____

20____

_____
_____
_____
_____

MARCH 7

20_____

_____

_____

_____

_____

20_____

_____

_____

_____

_____

20_____

_____

_____

_____

_____

20_____

_____

_____

_____

_____

20_____

_____

_____

_____

_____

"You better straighten up or we will be going to fist city." Lillian V. Fults

MARCH 8

20_____

_____
_____
_____
_____

20_____

_____
_____
_____
_____

20_____

_____
_____
_____
_____

20_____

_____
_____
_____
_____

20_____

_____
_____
_____
_____

MILEMARKERS

MARCH 9

20_____

_____
_____
_____
_____

20_____

_____
_____
_____
_____

20_____

_____
_____
_____

20_____

_____
_____
_____

20_____

_____
_____
_____

"The mind is a wonderful thing. It starts to work the minute you're born and never stops until you get up to speak in public." John Mason Brown

MARCH 10

20_____

_____

_____

_____

20_____

_____

_____

_____

_____

20_____

_____

_____

_____

_____

20_____

_____

_____

_____

_____

20_____

_____

_____

_____

_____

MARCH 11

20_____

_____
_____
_____
_____

20_____

_____
_____
_____
_____

20_____

_____
_____
_____
_____

20_____

_____
_____
_____
_____

20_____

_____
_____
_____
_____

"When you learn, teach. When you get, give."
Maya Angelou

MARCH 12

20_____

_____
_____
_____
_____

20_____

_____
_____
_____
_____

20_____

_____
_____
_____
_____

20_____

_____
_____
_____
_____

20_____

_____
_____
_____
_____

MILEMARKERS

MARCH 13

20_____

_____
_____
_____
_____

20_____

_____
_____
_____
_____

20_____

_____
_____
_____
_____

20_____

_____
_____
_____
_____

20_____

_____
_____
_____
_____

"Culture is like baking. Have ingredients, mix it up, and apply time and energy." Jerrod Murr

MARCH 14

20_____

_____
_____
_____
_____

20_____

_____
_____
_____
_____

20_____

_____
_____
_____
_____

20_____

_____
_____
_____
_____

20_____

_____
_____
_____
_____

MILEMARKERS

MARCH 15

20____

_____

_____

_____

_____

20____

_____

_____

_____

_____

20____

_____

_____

_____

_____

20____

_____

_____

_____

_____

20____

_____

_____

_____

_____

"Be sincere. Be brief. Be seated."
Franklin D. Roosevelt

MARCH 16

20_____

_____
_____
_____
_____

20_____

_____
_____
_____
_____

20_____

_____
_____
_____
_____

20_____

_____
_____
_____
_____

20_____

_____
_____
_____
_____

MILEMARKERS

MARCH 17

20_____

_____

_____

_____

_____

20_____

_____

_____

_____

_____

20_____

_____

_____

_____

_____

20_____

_____

_____

_____

_____

20_____

_____

_____

_____

_____

"Unhitch the wagon and put the ponies in the barn."
Toby Rowland

MARCH 18

20_____

_____

_____

_____

20_____

_____

_____

_____

20_____

_____

_____

_____

20_____

_____

_____

_____

20_____

_____

_____

_____

MILEMARKERS

MARCH 19

20_____

_____

_____

_____

_____

20_____

_____

_____

_____

_____

20_____

_____

_____

_____

_____

20_____

_____

_____

_____

_____

20_____

_____

_____

_____

_____

"Before you are a leader, success is all about yourself. When you become a leader, success is all about growing others." Jack Welch

MARCH 20

20_____

_____

_____

_____

_____

20_____

_____

_____

_____

_____

20_____

_____

_____

_____

_____

20_____

_____

_____

_____

_____

20_____

_____

_____

_____

_____

MILEMARKERS

MARCH 21

20____

_____
_____
_____
_____

20____

_____
_____
_____
_____

20____

_____
_____
_____
_____

20____

_____
_____
_____
_____

20____

_____
_____
_____
_____

"Today I will do what others won't, so tomorrow I can accomplish what others can't." Jerry Rice

MARCH 22

20_____

_____

_____

_____

_____

20_____

_____

_____

_____

_____

20_____

_____

_____

_____

_____

20_____

_____

_____

_____

_____

20_____

_____

_____

_____

_____

MARCH 23

20____

_____
_____
_____
_____

20____

_____
_____
_____
_____

20____

_____
_____
_____
_____

20____

_____
_____
_____
_____

20____

_____
_____
_____
_____

"The best revenge is massive success." Frank Sinatra

MARCH 24

20_____

_____
_____
_____
_____

20_____

_____
_____
_____
_____

20_____

_____
_____
_____
_____

20_____

_____
_____
_____
_____

20_____

_____
_____
_____
_____

MILEMARKERS

MARCH 25

20_____

_____
_____
_____
_____

20_____

_____
_____
_____
_____

20_____

_____
_____
_____
_____

20_____

_____
_____
_____
_____

20_____

_____
_____
_____

"Figure out what your boss wants and deliver. When they are successful, it's likely you will be too."
Deborah Reynolds

MARCH 26

20_____

_____

_____

_____

20_____

_____

_____

_____

20_____

_____

_____

_____

20_____

_____

_____

_____

20_____

_____

_____

_____

MARCH 27

20_____

_____
_____
_____
_____

20_____

_____
_____
_____
_____

20_____

_____
_____
_____
_____

20_____

_____
_____
_____
_____

20_____

_____
_____
_____
_____

"I love the smell of possibility in the morning."
Mel Robbins

MARCH 28

20_____

_____

_____

_____

_____

20_____

_____

_____

_____

_____

20_____

_____

_____

_____

_____

20_____

_____

_____

_____

_____

20_____

_____

_____

_____

_____

MARCH 29

20_____

_____

_____

_____

_____

20_____

_____

_____

_____

_____

20_____

_____

_____

_____

_____

20_____

_____

_____

_____

_____

20_____

_____

_____

_____

_____

"This is not a dress rehearsal, so if you want something – go get it!" Denise Preston Hunter

MARCH 30

20_____

_____

_____

_____

_____

20_____

_____

_____

_____

_____

20_____

_____

_____

_____

_____

20_____

_____

_____

_____

_____

20_____

_____

_____

_____

_____

MARCH 31

20_____

_____
_____
_____
_____

20_____

_____
_____
_____
_____

20_____

_____
_____
_____
_____

20_____

_____
_____
_____
_____

20_____

_____
_____
_____
_____

"When leaders learn and live good values, they make themselves more valuable." John C. Maxwell

Monthly Reflections...

My favorite book(s):

_____

_____

_____

_____

My favorite song(s):

_____

_____

_____

_____

My favorite memory:

_____

_____

_____

_____

"Take the mirror test: Are you better today than yesterday, are you growing or shrinking, are you engaged or disengaged?" Earl K. Reynolds

APRIL 1

20_____

_____
_____
_____
_____

20_____

_____
_____
_____
_____

20_____

_____
_____
_____
_____

20_____

_____
_____
_____
_____

20_____

_____
_____
_____
_____

"No matter where you go; no matter what the weather is, always bring sunshine with you." Peppa Pig

APRIL 2

20_____

_____
_____
_____
_____

20_____

_____
_____
_____
_____

20_____

_____
_____
_____
_____

20_____

_____
_____
_____
_____

20_____

_____
_____
_____
_____

APRIL 3

20_____

_____

_____

_____

_____

20_____

_____

_____

_____

_____

20_____

_____

_____

_____

_____

20_____

_____

_____

_____

_____

20_____

_____

_____

_____

_____

"The costs of your bad habits are in the future, the costs of your good habits are in the present." James Clear

APRIL 4

20_____

_____
_____
_____
_____

20_____

_____
_____
_____
_____

20_____

_____
_____
_____
_____

20_____

_____
_____
_____
_____

20_____

_____
_____
_____
_____

APRIL 5

20_____

_____
_____
_____
_____

20_____

_____
_____
_____
_____

20_____

_____
_____
_____
_____

20_____

_____
_____
_____
_____

20_____

_____
_____
_____
_____

*"It doesn't matter if you're a mentee or a mentor...
just be one."* Bruce Waller

APRIL 6

20_____

_____

_____

_____

_____

20_____

_____

_____

_____

_____

20_____

_____

_____

_____

_____

20_____

_____

_____

_____

_____

20_____

_____

_____

_____

_____

APRIL 7

20_____

_____
_____
_____
_____

20_____

_____
_____
_____
_____

20_____

_____
_____
_____
_____

20_____

_____
_____
_____
_____

20_____

_____
_____
_____
_____

"What comes easy won't last long, and what lasts long won't come easy!" Anonymous

APRIL 8

20_____

_____
_____
_____
_____

20_____

_____
_____
_____
_____

20_____

_____
_____
_____
_____

20_____

_____
_____
_____
_____

20_____

_____
_____
_____
_____

MILEMARKERS

APRIL 9

20_____

_____
_____
_____
_____

20_____

_____
_____
_____
_____

20_____

_____
_____
_____
_____

20_____

_____
_____
_____
_____

20_____

_____
_____
_____
_____

"The art is in the start." Steve Shallenberger

APRIL 10

20_____

_____

_____

_____

_____

20_____

_____

_____

_____

_____

20_____

_____

_____

_____

_____

20_____

_____

_____

_____

_____

20_____

_____

_____

_____

_____

MILEMARKERS

APRIL 11

20_____

_____

_____

_____

_____

20_____

_____

_____

_____

_____

20_____

_____

_____

_____

_____

20_____

_____

_____

_____

_____

20_____

_____

_____

_____

_____

"If you have the opportunity to do amazing things in your life, bring someone with you." Simon Sinek

APRIL 12

20_____

_____
_____
_____
_____

20_____

_____
_____
_____
_____

20_____

_____
_____
_____
_____

20_____

_____
_____
_____
_____

20_____

_____
_____
_____
_____

MILEMARKERS

APRIL 13

20_____

_____
_____
_____
_____

20_____

_____
_____
_____
_____

20_____

_____
_____
_____
_____

20_____

_____
_____
_____
_____

20_____

_____
_____
_____
_____

"The first step in leadership is not action, it's understanding." John W. Gardner

APRIL 14

20_____

_____
_____
_____
_____

20_____

_____
_____
_____
_____

20_____

_____
_____
_____
_____

20_____

_____
_____
_____
_____

20_____

_____
_____
_____
_____

MILEMARKERS

APRIL 15

20_____

_____

_____

_____

_____

20_____

_____

_____

_____

_____

20_____

_____

_____

_____

_____

20_____

_____

_____

_____

_____

20_____

_____

_____

_____

_____

"Your most important work is always ahead of you."
Tim Tebow

APRIL 16

20_____

_____
_____
_____
_____

20_____

_____
_____
_____
_____

20_____

_____
_____
_____
_____

20_____

_____
_____
_____
_____

20_____

_____
_____
_____
_____

MILEMARKERS

APRIL 17

20_____

_____

_____

_____

_____

20_____

_____

_____

_____

_____

20_____

_____

_____

_____

_____

20_____

_____

_____

_____

_____

20_____

_____

_____

_____

_____

"Gratitude, humility, and respect are three of the most important qualities you can have in life." Drew Brees

APRIL 18

20_____

_____
_____
_____
_____

20_____

_____
_____
_____
_____

20_____

_____
_____
_____
_____

20_____

_____
_____
_____
_____

20_____

_____
_____
_____
_____

MILEMARKERS

APRIL 19

20_____

_____

_____

_____

_____

20_____

_____

_____

_____

_____

20_____

_____

_____

_____

_____

20_____

_____

_____

_____

_____

20_____

_____

_____

_____

_____

"You will get all you want in life if you help enough other people get what they want." Zig Ziglar

APRIL 20

20_____

_____

_____

_____

_____

20_____

_____

_____

_____

_____

20_____

_____

_____

_____

_____

20_____

_____

_____

_____

_____

20_____

_____

_____

_____

_____

MILEMARKERS

APRIL 21

20_____

_____

_____

_____

_____

20_____

_____

_____

_____

_____

20_____

_____

_____

_____

_____

20_____

_____

_____

_____

_____

20_____

_____

_____

_____

_____

"Whatever you are, be a good one." Abraham Lincoln

APRIL 22

20_____

_____
_____
_____
_____

20_____

_____
_____
_____
_____

20_____

_____
_____
_____
_____

20_____

_____
_____
_____
_____

20_____

_____
_____
_____
_____

MILEMARKERS

APRIL 23

20_____

_____
_____
_____
_____

20_____

_____
_____
_____
_____

20_____

_____
_____
_____
_____

20_____

_____
_____
_____
_____

20_____

_____
_____
_____
_____

"We did not come to fear the future, we came to shape it."
Barack Obama

APRIL 24

20_____

_____
_____
_____
_____

20_____

_____
_____
_____
_____

20_____

_____
_____
_____
_____

20_____

_____
_____
_____
_____

20_____

_____
_____
_____
_____

APRIL 25

20_____

_____

_____

_____

_____

20_____

_____

_____

_____

_____

20_____

_____

_____

_____

_____

20_____

_____

_____

_____

_____

20_____

_____

_____

_____

_____

"Every expert was once a beginner."
Rutherford B. Hayes

APRIL 26

20_____

_____
_____
_____
_____

20_____

_____
_____
_____
_____

20_____

_____
_____
_____
_____

20_____

_____
_____
_____
_____

20_____

_____
_____
_____
_____

APRIL 27

20_____

_____
_____
_____
_____

20_____

_____
_____
_____
_____

20_____

_____
_____
_____
_____

20_____

_____
_____
_____
_____

20_____

_____
_____
_____

"Everybody needs four things in life:: Something to do, someone to love, someone to believe in and something to hope for." Lou Holtz

APRIL 28

20_____

_____
_____
_____
_____

20_____

_____
_____
_____
_____

20_____

_____
_____
_____
_____

20_____

_____
_____
_____
_____

20_____

_____
_____
_____
_____

APRIL 29

20_____

_____

_____

_____

_____

20_____

_____

_____

_____

_____

20_____

_____

_____

_____

_____

20_____

_____

_____

_____

_____

20_____

_____

_____

_____

_____

"Your people are your company's greatest selling point. Give them a voice." Craig Fisher

APRIL 30

20_____

_____

_____

_____

_____

20_____

_____

_____

_____

_____

20_____

_____

_____

_____

_____

20_____

_____

_____

_____

_____

20_____

_____

_____

_____

_____

Monthly Reflections...

Something I am really proud of accomplishing:

_____

_____

_____

_____

A challenge I had to overcome:

_____

_____

_____

_____

My mantra or creed:

_____

_____

_____

_____

"Respect and forgiveness are just a waste of time,
unless we practice them." Jack Waller

MAY 1

20_____

_____
_____
_____
_____

20_____

_____
_____
_____
_____

20_____

_____
_____
_____
_____

20_____

_____
_____
_____
_____

20_____

_____
_____
_____
_____

"You'll become more interesting when you become more interested." Carmine Gallo

MAY 2

20_____

_____
_____
_____
_____

20_____

_____
_____
_____
_____

20_____

_____
_____
_____
_____

20_____

_____
_____
_____
_____

20_____

_____
_____
_____
_____

MILEMARKERS

MAY 3

20_____

_____
_____
_____
_____

20_____

_____
_____
_____
_____

20_____

_____
_____
_____
_____

20_____

_____
_____
_____
_____

20_____

_____
_____
_____
_____

*"Those we love don't go away,
they walk beside us every day."* Anonymous

MAY 4

20_____

_____

_____

_____

_____

20_____

_____

_____

_____

_____

20_____

_____

_____

_____

_____

20_____

_____

_____

_____

_____

20_____

_____

_____

_____

_____

MAY 5

20_____

_____
_____
_____
_____

20_____

_____
_____
_____
_____

20_____

_____
_____
_____
_____

20_____

_____
_____
_____
_____

20_____

_____
_____
_____
_____

"If you want to walk on water, you've got to get out of the boat." John Ortberg

MAY 6

20_____

_____
_____
_____
_____

20_____

_____
_____
_____
_____

20_____

_____
_____
_____
_____

20_____

_____
_____
_____
_____

20_____

_____
_____
_____
_____

MAY 7

20_____

_____

_____

_____

_____

20_____

_____

_____

_____

_____

20_____

_____

_____

_____

_____

20_____

_____

_____

_____

_____

20_____

_____

_____

_____

_____

"If you want to go fast, go alone, but if you want to go far, go together." African Proverb

MAY 8

20_____

_____
_____
_____
_____

20_____

_____
_____
_____
_____

20_____

_____
_____
_____
_____

20_____

_____
_____
_____
_____

20_____

_____
_____
_____
_____

MAY 9

20_____

_____

_____

_____

_____

20_____

_____

_____

_____

_____

20_____

_____

_____

_____

_____

20_____

_____

_____

_____

_____

20_____

_____

_____

_____

_____

"The best part about success is sharing with others."
Michael Gonzales

MAY 10

20_____

_____
_____
_____
_____

20_____

_____
_____
_____
_____

20_____

_____
_____
_____
_____

20_____

_____
_____
_____
_____

20_____

_____
_____
_____
_____

MAY 11

20_____

_____
_____
_____
_____

20_____

_____
_____
_____
_____

20_____

_____
_____
_____
_____

20_____

_____
_____
_____
_____

20_____

_____
_____
_____
_____

"Appreciate the coaches that teach you about life.
Those lessons will last long after you're done playing
the game." Michael Schlact

MAY 12

20_____

_____
_____
_____
_____

20_____

_____
_____
_____
_____

20_____

_____
_____
_____
_____

20_____

_____
_____
_____
_____

20_____

_____
_____
_____
_____

MAY 13

20_____

_____
_____
_____
_____

20_____

_____
_____
_____
_____

20_____

_____
_____
_____
_____

20_____

_____
_____
_____
_____

20_____

_____
_____
_____
_____

"Always operate in a mindset of gratitude, our mind believes what we think and our path to success starts with our attitude." Lynne Stewart

MAY 14

20_____

_____
_____
_____
_____

20_____

_____
_____
_____
_____

20_____

_____
_____
_____
_____

20_____

_____
_____
_____
_____

20_____

_____
_____
_____
_____

MILEMARKERS

MAY 15

20_____

_____

_____

_____

_____

20_____

_____

_____

_____

_____

20_____

_____

_____

_____

_____

20_____

_____

_____

_____

_____

20_____

_____

_____

_____

_____

"Commitment is not a feeling, it's an action."
Gian Paul Gonzalez

MAY 16

20_____

_____
_____
_____
_____

20_____

_____
_____
_____
_____

20_____

_____
_____
_____
_____

20_____

_____
_____
_____
_____

20_____

_____
_____
_____
_____

MAY 17

20_____

_____

_____

_____

_____

20_____

_____

_____

_____

_____

20_____

_____

_____

_____

_____

20_____

_____

_____

_____

_____

20_____

_____

_____

_____

_____

"I alone cannot change the world, but I can cast a stone across the waters to create many ripples."
Mother Teresa

MAY 18

20_____

_____
_____
_____
_____

20_____

_____
_____
_____
_____

20_____

_____
_____
_____
_____

20_____

_____
_____
_____
_____

20_____

_____
_____
_____
_____

MAY 19

20_____

_____
_____
_____
_____

20_____

_____
_____
_____
_____

20_____

_____
_____
_____
_____

20_____

_____
_____
_____
_____

20_____

_____
_____
_____
_____

"If you have only one smile in you, give it to the people you love." Maya Angelou

MAY 20

20_____

_____
_____
_____
_____

20_____

_____
_____
_____
_____

20_____

_____
_____
_____
_____

20_____

_____
_____
_____
_____

20_____

_____
_____
_____
_____

MILEMARKERS

MAY 21

20_____

_____

_____

_____

_____

20_____

_____

_____

_____

_____

20_____

_____

_____

_____

_____

20_____

_____

_____

_____

_____

20_____

_____

_____

_____

_____

"If you want to receive a call, then you might want to make one first." Dana Maria Waller

MAY 22

20_____

_____
_____
_____
_____

20_____

_____
_____
_____
_____

20_____

_____
_____
_____
_____

20_____

_____
_____
_____
_____

20_____

_____
_____
_____
_____

MILEMARKERS

MAY 23

20_____

_____

_____

_____

_____

20_____

_____

_____

_____

_____

20_____

_____

_____

_____

_____

20_____

_____

_____

_____

_____

20_____

_____

_____

_____

_____

"Everything you want is on the other side of fear."
Jack Canfield

MAY 24

20_____

_____
_____
_____
_____

20_____

_____
_____
_____
_____

20_____

_____
_____
_____
_____

20_____

_____
_____
_____
_____

20_____

_____
_____
_____
_____

MILEMARKERS

MAY 25

20_____

_____

_____

_____

_____

20_____

_____

_____

_____

_____

20_____

_____

_____

_____

_____

20_____

_____

_____

_____

_____

20_____

_____

_____

_____

_____

*"Write. Rewrite. When not writing or rewriting, read.
I know no shortcuts."* Larry L. King

MAY 26

20_____

_____
_____
_____
_____

20_____

_____
_____
_____
_____

20_____

_____
_____
_____
_____

20_____

_____
_____
_____
_____

20_____

_____
_____
_____
_____

MAY 27

20_____

_____
_____
_____
_____

20_____

_____
_____
_____
_____

20_____

_____
_____
_____
_____

20_____

_____
_____
_____
_____

20_____

_____
_____
_____
_____

"Don't wait. The timing will never be just right."
Napoleon Hill

MAY 28

20_____

20_____

20_____

20_____

20_____

MILEMARKERS

MAY 29

20_____

_____
_____
_____
_____

20_____

_____
_____
_____
_____

20_____

_____
_____
_____
_____

20_____

_____
_____
_____
_____

20_____

_____
_____
_____
_____

"A brother is born for times of adversity."
King Solomon

MAY 30

20_____

_____
_____
_____
_____

20_____

_____
_____
_____
_____

20_____

_____
_____
_____
_____

20_____

_____
_____
_____
_____

20_____

_____
_____
_____
_____

MAY 31

20_____

_____

_____

_____

_____

20_____

_____

_____

_____

_____

20_____

_____

_____

_____

_____

20_____

_____

_____

_____

_____

20_____

_____

_____

_____

_____

"It is the experience collected in our lives that is of utmost importance to our lives and careers."
Adrianne Court

Monthly Reflections...

Someone who inspired me:

_____

_____

_____

Something I would like to learn:

_____

_____

_____

Some of my goals:

_____

_____

_____

_____

_____

_____

"Do all the good you can. By all the means you can. In all the ways you can. In all the places you can. At all the times you can. To all the people you can. As long as ever you can." John Wesley

JUNE 1

20_____

_____

_____

_____

_____

20_____

_____

_____

_____

_____

20_____

_____

_____

_____

_____

20_____

_____

_____

_____

_____

20_____

_____

_____

_____

_____

"You will soon break the bow if you keep it always stretched." Norman Vincent Peale

JUNE 2

20____

_____

_____

_____

_____

20____

_____

_____

_____

_____

20____

_____

_____

_____

_____

20____

_____

_____

_____

_____

20____

_____

_____

_____

_____

JUNE 3

20_____

_____

_____

_____

_____

20_____

_____

_____

_____

_____

20_____

_____

_____

_____

_____

20_____

_____

_____

_____

_____

20_____

_____

_____

_____

_____

"Coaching people based on their potential will help them rise to the highest level." Troy Aikman

JUNE 4

20_____

_____
_____
_____
_____

20_____

_____
_____
_____
_____

20_____

_____
_____
_____
_____

20_____

_____
_____
_____
_____

20_____

_____
_____
_____
_____

JUNE 5

20_____

_____

_____

_____

_____

20_____

_____

_____

_____

_____

20_____

_____

_____

_____

_____

20_____

_____

_____

_____

_____

20_____

_____

_____

_____

_____

"Never risk more than you can afford to lose."
Jack H. Thornton

JUNE 6

20_____

_____
_____
_____
_____

20_____

_____
_____
_____
_____

20_____

_____
_____
_____
_____

20_____

_____
_____
_____
_____

20_____

_____
_____
_____
_____

JUNE 7

20_____

_____
_____
_____
_____

20_____

_____
_____
_____
_____

20_____

_____
_____
_____
_____

20_____

_____
_____
_____
_____

20_____

_____
_____
_____
_____

"If I cannot do great things, I can do small things in a great way." Martin Luther King Jr.

JUNE 8

20_____

_____
_____
_____
_____

20_____

_____
_____
_____
_____

20_____

_____
_____
_____
_____

20_____

_____
_____
_____
_____

20_____

_____
_____
_____
_____

JUNE 9

20____

_____
_____
_____
_____

20____

_____
_____
_____
_____

20____

_____
_____
_____
_____

20____

_____
_____
_____
_____

20____

_____
_____
_____
_____

"Learn to listen, listen to learn." Tom Izzo

JUNE 10

20_____

_____
_____
_____
_____

20_____

_____
_____
_____
_____

20_____

_____
_____
_____
_____

20_____

_____
_____
_____
_____

20_____

_____
_____
_____
_____

JUNE 11

20____

_____
_____
_____
_____

20____

_____
_____
_____
_____

20____

_____
_____
_____
_____

20____

_____
_____
_____
_____

20____

_____
_____
_____
_____

"Just keep going. Everybody gets better if they keep at it." Ted Williams

JUNE 12

20_____

_____
_____
_____
_____

20_____

_____
_____
_____
_____

20_____

_____
_____
_____

20_____

_____
_____
_____

20_____

_____
_____
_____
_____

JUNE 13

20_____

_____
_____
_____
_____

20_____

_____
_____
_____
_____

20_____

_____
_____
_____
_____

20_____

_____
_____
_____
_____

20_____

_____
_____
_____
_____

"Humility doesn't mean you think less of yourself, but that you think of yourself less." Max Lucado

JUNE 14

20_____

_____

_____

_____

_____

20_____

_____

_____

_____

_____

20_____

_____

_____

_____

_____

20_____

_____

_____

_____

_____

20_____

_____

_____

_____

_____

JUNE 15

20____

_____

_____

_____

_____

20____

_____

_____

_____

_____

20____

_____

_____

_____

_____

20____

_____

_____

_____

_____

20____

_____

_____

_____

_____

"You never meet anyone by accident, chance or coincidence."
Diana Meisenhelter

JUNE 16

20_____

_____
_____
_____
_____

20_____

_____
_____
_____
_____

20_____

_____
_____
_____
_____

20_____

_____
_____
_____
_____

20_____

_____
_____
_____
_____

MILEMARKERS

JUNE 17

20_____

_____

_____

_____

_____

20_____

_____

_____

_____

_____

20_____

_____

_____

_____

_____

20_____

_____

_____

_____

_____

20_____

_____

_____

_____

_____

"Some men see things as they are and ask why, I dream of things that never were and ask why not."
Robert Kennedy

JUNE 18

20_____

_____
_____
_____
_____

20_____

_____
_____
_____
_____

20_____

_____
_____
_____
_____

20_____

_____
_____
_____
_____

20_____

_____
_____
_____
_____

JUNE 19

20_____

_____
_____
_____
_____

20_____

_____
_____
_____
_____

20_____

_____
_____
_____
_____

20_____

_____
_____
_____
_____

20_____

_____
_____
_____
_____

"The customer experience will never exceed the employee experience." Tony Bridwell

JUNE 20

20_____

_____

_____

_____

_____

20_____

_____

_____

_____

_____

20_____

_____

_____

_____

_____

20_____

_____

_____

_____

_____

20_____

_____

_____

_____

_____

JUNE 21

20_____

_____
_____
_____
_____

20_____

_____
_____
_____
_____

20_____

_____
_____
_____
_____

20_____

_____
_____
_____
_____

20_____

_____
_____
_____
_____

"It's what you learn after you know it all that counts."
John Wooden

JUNE 22

20_____

_____
_____
_____
_____

20_____

_____
_____
_____
_____

20_____

_____
_____
_____
_____

20_____

_____
_____
_____
_____

20_____

_____
_____
_____
_____

MILEMARKERS

JUNE 23

20_____

_____
_____
_____
_____

20_____

_____
_____
_____
_____

20_____

_____
_____
_____
_____

20_____

_____
_____
_____
_____

20_____

_____
_____
_____
_____

"It's easier to stay in shape than it is to get in shape."
Will Smith

JUNE 24

20_____

_____
_____
_____
_____

20_____

_____
_____
_____
_____

20_____

_____
_____
_____
_____

20_____

_____
_____
_____
_____

20_____

_____
_____
_____
_____

MILEMARKERS

JUNE 25

20_____

_____

_____

_____

20_____

_____

_____

_____

20_____

_____

_____

_____

20_____

_____

_____

_____

20_____

_____

_____

_____

"We make a living by what we get, but we make a life by what we give." Winston Churchill

JUNE 26

20_____

_____

_____

_____

_____

20_____

_____

_____

_____

_____

20_____

_____

_____

_____

_____

20_____

_____

_____

_____

_____

20_____

_____

_____

_____

_____

JUNE 27

20_____

_____
_____
_____
_____

20_____

_____
_____
_____
_____

20_____

_____
_____
_____
_____

20_____

_____
_____
_____
_____

20_____

_____
_____
_____
_____

"Effort needs no talent." Rufus Alexander

JUNE 28

20_____

_____
_____
_____
_____

20_____

_____
_____
_____
_____

20_____

_____
_____
_____
_____

20_____

_____
_____
_____
_____

20_____

_____
_____
_____
_____

JUNE 29

20_____

20_____

20_____

20_____

20_____

"If I can, I will." Margaret Lee Parks

JUNE 30

20_____

_____

_____

_____

_____

20_____

_____

_____

_____

_____

20_____

_____

_____

_____

_____

20_____

_____

_____

_____

_____

20_____

_____

_____

_____

_____

MILEMARKERS

Monthly Reflections...

Places I would like to visit:

_____

_____

_____

_____

People I would like to meet:

_____

_____

_____

_____

My favorite hobbies:

_____

_____

_____

_____

"Before you can achieve the kind of life you want you must think, act, talk, and conduct yourself in all of your affairs as would the person you wish to become."
Earl Nightingale

JULY 1

20____

_____
_____
_____
_____

20____

_____
_____
_____
_____

20____

_____
_____
_____
_____

20____

_____
_____
_____
_____

20____

_____
_____
_____
_____

"Give me six hours to chop down a tree and I will spend the first four sharpening the axe." Abraham Lincoln

JULY 2

20_____

_____

_____

_____

_____

20_____

_____

_____

_____

_____

20_____

_____

_____

_____

_____

20_____

_____

_____

_____

_____

20_____

_____

_____

_____

_____

JULY 3

20_____

_____

_____

_____

_____

20_____

_____

_____

_____

_____

20_____

_____

_____

_____

_____

20_____

_____

_____

_____

_____

20_____

_____

_____

_____

_____

"Life all comes down to a few moments.
This is one of them." Bud Fox

JULY 4

20_____

20_____

20_____

20_____

20_____

JULY 5

20_____

_____
_____
_____
_____

20_____

_____
_____
_____
_____

20_____

_____
_____
_____
_____

20_____

_____
_____
_____
_____

20_____

_____
_____
_____
_____

"Feedback is a gift." Shelley Zajic

JULY 6

20_____

_____
_____
_____
_____

20_____

_____
_____
_____
_____

20_____

_____
_____
_____
_____

20_____

_____
_____
_____
_____

20_____

_____
_____
_____
_____

JULY 7

20_____

_____
_____
_____
_____

20_____

_____
_____
_____
_____

20_____

_____
_____
_____
_____

20_____

_____
_____
_____
_____

20_____

_____
_____
_____
_____

"The secret of getting ahead is getting started."
Mark Twain

JULY 8

20_____

_____
_____
_____
_____

20_____

_____
_____
_____
_____

20_____

_____
_____
_____
_____

20_____

_____
_____
_____
_____

20_____

_____
_____
_____
_____

MILEMARKERS

JULY 9

20_____

_____
_____
_____
_____

20_____

_____
_____
_____
_____

20_____

_____
_____
_____
_____

20_____

_____
_____
_____
_____

20_____

_____
_____
_____
_____

"It's all about knowing your formula for winning."
Lincoln Riley

JULY 10

20_____

_____
_____
_____
_____

20_____

_____
_____
_____
_____

20_____

_____
_____
_____
_____

20_____

_____
_____
_____
_____

20_____

_____
_____
_____
_____

MILEMARKERS

JULY 11

20_____

_____

20_____

_____

20_____

_____

20_____

_____

20_____

_____

"Ask yourself 3 times a day what's important to you, then have the courage to build your life around your answer."
Tom Watson

JULY 12

20_____

_____

_____

_____

_____

20_____

_____

_____

_____

_____

20_____

_____

_____

_____

_____

20_____

_____

_____

_____

_____

20_____

_____

_____

_____

_____

JULY 13

20_____

_____
_____
_____
_____

20_____

_____
_____
_____
_____

20_____

_____
_____
_____
_____

20_____

_____
_____
_____
_____

20_____

_____
_____
_____
_____

"The number one factor in leadership is caring for others." Steve Browne

JULY 14

20_____

_____

_____

_____

_____

20_____

_____

_____

_____

_____

20_____

_____

_____

_____

_____

20_____

_____

_____

_____

_____

20_____

_____

_____

_____

_____

JULY 15

20____

_____
_____
_____
_____

20____

_____
_____
_____
_____

20____

_____
_____
_____
_____

20____

_____
_____
_____
_____

20____

_____
_____
_____
_____

"Don't ever look at the empty seats." Charlie Daniels

JULY 16

20_____

_____
_____
_____
_____

20_____

_____
_____
_____
_____

20_____

_____
_____
_____
_____

20_____

_____
_____
_____
_____

20_____

_____
_____
_____
_____

JULY 17

20_____

_____
_____
_____
_____

20_____

_____
_____
_____
_____

20_____

_____
_____
_____
_____

20_____

_____
_____
_____
_____

20_____

_____
_____
_____
_____

"I'm not the smartest fellow in the world, but I sure can pick smart colleagues." Franklin D Roosevelt

JULY 18

20_____

_____

_____

_____

_____

20_____

_____

_____

_____

_____

20_____

_____

_____

_____

_____

20_____

_____

_____

_____

_____

20_____

_____

_____

_____

_____

JULY 19

20____

_____
_____
_____
_____

20____

_____
_____
_____
_____

20____

_____
_____
_____
_____

20____

_____
_____
_____
_____

20____

_____
_____
_____
_____

"Be yourself, Know yourself, Accept yourself."
Mike Martin

JULY 20

20_____

_____
_____
_____
_____

20_____

_____
_____
_____
_____

20_____

_____
_____
_____
_____

20_____

_____
_____
_____
_____

20_____

_____
_____
_____
_____

JULY 21

20_____

_____
_____
_____
_____

20_____

_____
_____
_____
_____

20_____

_____
_____
_____
_____

20_____

_____
_____
_____
_____

20_____

_____
_____
_____
_____

"Comparison is the thief of joy!" Theodore Roosevelt

JULY 22

20____

_____

20____

_____

20____

_____

20____

_____

20____

_____

JULY 23

20_____

_____
_____
_____
_____

20_____

_____
_____
_____
_____

20_____

_____
_____
_____
_____

20_____

_____
_____
_____
_____

20_____

_____
_____
_____
_____

"The bigger the why, the easier the how!" Jim Rohn

JULY 24

20_____

_____
_____
_____
_____

20_____

_____
_____
_____
_____

20_____

_____
_____
_____
_____

20_____

_____
_____
_____
_____

20_____

_____
_____
_____
_____

JULY 25

20_____

_____
_____
_____
_____

20_____

_____
_____
_____
_____

20_____

_____
_____
_____
_____

20_____

_____
_____
_____
_____

20_____

_____
_____
_____
_____

"Invest in the people zone for the biggest return in your career and in life." Bruce Waller

JULY 26

20_____

_____
_____
_____
_____

20_____

_____
_____
_____
_____

20_____

_____
_____
_____
_____

20_____

_____
_____
_____
_____

20_____

_____
_____
_____
_____

MILEMARKERS

JULY 27

20_____

_____
_____
_____
_____

20_____

_____
_____
_____
_____

20_____

_____
_____
_____
_____

20_____

_____
_____
_____
_____

20_____

_____
_____
_____
_____

"Young people need models, not critics."
John Wooden

JULY 28

20_____

_____
_____
_____
_____

20_____

_____
_____
_____
_____

20_____

_____
_____
_____
_____

20_____

_____
_____
_____
_____

20_____

_____
_____
_____
_____

MILEMARKERS

JULY 29

20_____

_____
_____
_____
_____

20_____

_____
_____
_____
_____

20_____

_____
_____
_____
_____

20_____

_____
_____
_____
_____

20_____

_____
_____
_____
_____

"Know where your lifelines are." Kim Pisciotta

JULY 30

20_____

_____
_____
_____
_____

20_____

_____
_____
_____
_____

20_____

_____
_____
_____
_____

20_____

_____
_____
_____
_____

20_____

_____
_____
_____
_____

MILEMARKERS

JULY 31

20_____

_____
_____
_____
_____

20_____

_____
_____
_____
_____

20_____

_____
_____
_____
_____

20_____

_____
_____
_____
_____

20_____

_____
_____
_____
_____

"The best way to find yourself is to lose yourself in the service of others." Mahatma Gandhi

Monthly Reflections...

The best advice I have ever received:

_____

_____

_____

_____

_____

Advice I'd like to share with others:

_____

_____

_____

_____

_____

My favorite quote:

_____

_____

_____

_____

*"Being healthy requires focus on all aspects of health,
including mental and physical, for optimal results."*
Allison Rezentes

AUGUST 1

20_____

_____
_____
_____
_____

20_____

_____
_____
_____
_____

20_____

_____
_____
_____
_____

20_____

_____
_____
_____
_____

20_____

_____
_____
_____
_____

"Flowers bloom in adversity." Lily Huff

AUGUST 2

20_____

_____

_____

_____

_____

20_____

_____

_____

_____

_____

20_____

_____

_____

_____

_____

20_____

_____

_____

_____

_____

20_____

_____

_____

_____

_____

AUGUST 3

20_____

_____
_____
_____
_____

20_____

_____
_____
_____
_____

20_____

_____
_____
_____
_____

20_____

_____
_____
_____
_____

20_____

_____
_____
_____
_____

"It's not how you start, but how you finish."
Mark Waller

AUGUST 4

20_____

_____
_____
_____
_____

20_____

_____
_____
_____
_____

20_____

_____
_____
_____
_____

20_____

_____
_____
_____
_____

20_____

_____
_____
_____
_____

MILEMARKERS

AUGUST 5

20_____

_____
_____
_____
_____

20_____

_____
_____
_____
_____

20_____

_____
_____
_____
_____

20_____

_____
_____
_____
_____

20_____

_____
_____
_____
_____

"Perfection is not attainable, but if we chase perfection we can catch excellence." Vince Lombardi

AUGUST 6

20_____

_____
_____
_____
_____

20_____

_____
_____
_____
_____

20_____

_____
_____
_____
_____

20_____

_____
_____
_____
_____

20_____

_____
_____
_____
_____

MILEMARKERS

AUGUST 7

20_____

_____
_____
_____
_____

20_____

_____
_____
_____
_____

20_____

_____
_____
_____
_____

20_____

_____
_____
_____
_____

20_____

_____
_____
_____
_____

"It's hotter than blue blazes out here." Dewey Ivey

AUGUST 8

20_____

_____
_____
_____
_____

20_____

_____
_____
_____
_____

20_____

_____
_____
_____
_____

20_____

_____
_____
_____
_____

20_____

_____
_____
_____
_____

MILEMARKERS

AUGUST 9

20_____

_____
_____
_____
_____

20_____

_____
_____
_____
_____

20_____

_____
_____
_____
_____

20_____

_____
_____
_____
_____

20_____

_____
_____
_____
_____

"Your network is your net worth." Darren Hardy

AUGUST 10

20_____

_____
_____
_____
_____

20_____

_____
_____
_____
_____

20_____

_____
_____
_____
_____

20_____

_____
_____
_____
_____

20_____

_____
_____
_____
_____

AUGUST 11

20_____

_____

_____

_____

_____

20_____

_____

_____

_____

_____

20_____

_____

_____

_____

_____

20_____

_____

_____

_____

_____

20_____

_____

_____

_____

_____

"Nobody who ever gave his best regretted it."
George Halas

AUGUST 12

20_____

_____
_____
_____
_____

20_____

_____
_____
_____
_____

20_____

_____
_____
_____
_____

20_____

_____
_____
_____
_____

20_____

_____
_____
_____
_____

AUGUST 13

20_____

_____

_____

_____

_____

20_____

_____

_____

_____

_____

20_____

_____

_____

_____

_____

20_____

_____

_____

_____

_____

20_____

_____

_____

_____

_____

"Love is the force that ignites the spirit and binds teams together." Phil Jackson

AUGUST 14

20_____

_____
_____
_____
_____

20_____

_____
_____
_____
_____

20_____

_____
_____
_____
_____

20_____

_____
_____
_____
_____

20_____

_____
_____
_____
_____

AUGUST 15

20_____

_____
_____
_____
_____

20_____

_____
_____
_____
_____

20_____

_____
_____
_____
_____

20_____

_____
_____
_____
_____

20_____

_____
_____
_____
_____

"Preparation is the key to success."
Alexander Graham Bell

AUGUST 16

20____

_____
_____
_____
_____

20____

_____
_____
_____
_____

20____

_____
_____
_____
_____

20____

_____
_____
_____
_____

20____

_____
_____
_____
_____

AUGUST 17

20____

_____
_____
_____
_____

20____

_____
_____
_____
_____

20____

_____
_____
_____
_____

20____

_____
_____
_____
_____

20____

_____
_____
_____
_____

"If I have seen further, it is by standing upon the shoulders of giants." Isaac Newton

AUGUST 18

20_____

_____
_____
_____
_____

20_____

_____
_____
_____
_____

20_____

_____
_____
_____
_____

20_____

_____
_____
_____
_____

20_____

_____
_____
_____
_____

AUGUST 19

20_____

_____
_____
_____
_____

20_____

_____
_____
_____
_____

20_____

_____
_____
_____
_____

20_____

_____
_____
_____
_____

20_____

_____
_____
_____
_____

"Make each day your masterpiece." John Wooden

AUGUST 20

20_____

_____
_____
_____
_____

20_____

_____
_____
_____
_____

20_____

_____
_____
_____
_____

20_____

_____
_____
_____
_____

20_____

_____
_____
_____
_____

AUGUST 21

20_____

_____
_____
_____
_____

20_____

_____
_____
_____
_____

20_____

_____
_____
_____
_____

20_____

_____
_____
_____
_____

20_____

_____
_____
_____
_____

"Always keep your character and integrity at the heart of all decisions." Dr. Gayle Stinson

AUGUST 22

20_____

_____
_____
_____
_____

20_____

_____
_____
_____
_____

20_____

_____
_____
_____
_____

20_____

_____
_____
_____
_____

20_____

_____
_____
_____
_____

MILEMARKERS

AUGUST 23

20_____

_____

_____

_____

_____

20_____

_____

_____

_____

_____

20_____

_____

_____

_____

_____

20_____

_____

_____

_____

_____

20_____

_____

_____

_____

_____

"The only thing we have to fear is fear itself."
Franklin D. Roosevelt

AUGUST 24

20_____

_____

_____

_____

_____

20_____

_____

_____

_____

_____

20_____

_____

_____

_____

_____

20_____

_____

_____

_____

_____

20_____

_____

_____

_____

_____

AUGUST 25

20____

_____
_____
_____
_____

20____

_____
_____
_____
_____

20____

_____
_____
_____
_____

20____

_____
_____
_____
_____

20____

_____
_____
_____
_____

"Every single day in every walk of life, ordinary people accomplish extraordinary things." Jim Valvano

AUGUST 26

20_____

_____
_____
_____
_____

20_____

_____
_____
_____
_____

20_____

_____
_____
_____
_____

20_____

_____
_____
_____
_____

20_____

_____
_____
_____
_____

AUGUST 27

20_____

_____

_____

_____

_____

20_____

_____

_____

_____

_____

20_____

_____

_____

_____

_____

20_____

_____

_____

_____

_____

20_____

_____

_____

_____

_____

*"Be humble enough to learn from everyone you meet
and every situation you encounter."* Dave Nelson

AUGUST 28

20_____

_____

_____

_____

_____

20_____

_____

_____

_____

_____

20_____

_____

_____

_____

_____

20_____

_____

_____

_____

_____

20_____

_____

_____

_____

_____

AUGUST 29

20_____

_____
_____
_____
_____

20_____

_____
_____
_____
_____

20_____

_____
_____
_____
_____

20_____

_____
_____
_____
_____

20_____

_____
_____
_____
_____

"You never get a second chance to make a first impression." Will Rogers

AUGUST 30

20_____

_____
_____
_____
_____

20_____

_____
_____
_____
_____

20_____

_____
_____
_____
_____

20_____

_____
_____
_____
_____

20_____

_____
_____
_____
_____

AUGUST 31

20_____

_____
_____
_____
_____

20_____

_____
_____
_____
_____

20_____

_____
_____
_____
_____

20_____

_____
_____
_____
_____

20_____

_____
_____
_____
_____

"A tiger hunts best when he's hungry." Phil Knight

Monthly Reflections...

Favorite movie(s):

_____

_____

_____

_____

Favorite sports team(s):

_____

_____

_____

_____

Favorite drink(s):

_____

_____

_____

_____

"Inaction breeds doubt and fear. Action breeds
confidence and courage. If you want to conquer fear, do
not sit home and think about it. Go out and get busy."
Dale Carnegie

SEPTEMBER 1

20_____

_____
_____
_____
_____

20_____

_____
_____
_____
_____

20_____

_____
_____
_____
_____

20_____

_____
_____
_____
_____

20_____

_____
_____
_____
_____

"Your success in the next 5 years will be determined by the books you read and the people you meet." Jim Rohn

SEPTEMBER 2

20_____

_____
_____
_____
_____

20_____

_____
_____
_____
_____

20_____

_____
_____
_____
_____

20_____

_____
_____
_____
_____

20_____

_____
_____
_____
_____

MILEMARKERS

SEPTEMBER 3

20_____

_____
_____
_____
_____

20_____

_____
_____
_____
_____

20_____

_____
_____
_____
_____

20_____

_____
_____
_____
_____

20_____

_____
_____
_____
_____

"We should always have dreams." Herb Brooks

SEPTEMBER 4

20_____

_____
_____
_____
_____

20_____

_____
_____
_____
_____

20_____

_____
_____
_____
_____

20_____

_____
_____
_____
_____

20_____

_____
_____
_____
_____

SEPTEMBER 5

20_____

_____

_____

_____

_____

20_____

_____

_____

_____

_____

20_____

_____

_____

_____

_____

20_____

_____

_____

_____

_____

20_____

_____

_____

_____

_____

"It is easier to resist at the beginning than at the end."
Leonardo da Vinci

SEPTEMBER 6

20____

_____
_____
_____
_____

20____

_____
_____
_____
_____

20____

_____
_____
_____
_____

20____

_____
_____
_____
_____

20____

_____
_____
_____
_____

SEPTEMBER 7

20_____

_____

_____

_____

_____

20_____

_____

_____

_____

_____

20_____

_____

_____

_____

_____

20_____

_____

_____

_____

_____

20_____

_____

_____

_____

_____

"The only thing worse than being blind is having sight but no vision." Helen Keller

SEPTEMBER 8

20_____

_____
_____
_____
_____

20_____

_____
_____
_____
_____

20_____

_____
_____
_____
_____

20_____

_____
_____
_____
_____

20_____

_____
_____
_____
_____

MILEMARKERS

SEPTEMBER 9

20____

_____
_____
_____
_____

20____

_____
_____
_____
_____

20____

_____
_____
_____
_____

20____

_____
_____
_____
_____

20____

_____
_____
_____
_____

"When you see obstacles, start looking for solutions."
Deanna Huff

SEPTEMBER 10

20_____

_____
_____
_____
_____

20_____

_____
_____
_____
_____

20_____

_____
_____
_____
_____

20_____

_____
_____
_____
_____

20_____

_____
_____
_____
_____

SEPTEMBER 11

20_____

_____

_____

_____

_____

20_____

_____

_____

_____

_____

20_____

_____

_____

_____

_____

20_____

_____

_____

_____

_____

20_____

_____

_____

_____

_____

"In the time of darkest defeat, victory may be nearest."
William McKinley

SEPTEMBER 12

20_____

_____
_____
_____
_____

20_____

_____
_____
_____
_____

20_____

_____
_____
_____
_____

20_____

_____
_____
_____
_____

20_____

_____
_____
_____
_____

SEPTEMBER 13

20_____

20_____

20_____

20_____

20_____

*"Whether you think you can, or you think you can't –
you're right."* Henry Ford

SEPTEMBER 14

20_____

_____
_____
_____
_____

20_____

_____
_____
_____
_____

20_____

_____
_____
_____
_____

20_____

_____
_____
_____
_____

20_____

_____
_____
_____
_____

SEPTEMBER 15

20_____

_____
_____
_____
_____

20_____

_____
_____
_____
_____

20_____

_____
_____
_____
_____

20_____

_____
_____
_____
_____

20_____

_____
_____
_____
_____

"Not everything that counts can be counted, and not everything that can be counted counts." Albert Einstein

SEPTEMBER 16

20_____

20_____

20_____

20_____

20_____

SEPTEMBER 17

20_____

20_____

20_____

20_____

20_____

"To be good, and to do good, is all we have to do."
John Adams

SEPTEMBER 18

20_____

_____
_____
_____
_____

20_____

_____
_____
_____
_____

20_____

_____
_____
_____
_____

20_____

_____
_____
_____
_____

20_____

_____
_____
_____
_____

MILEMARKERS

SEPTEMBER 19

20_____

_____

_____

_____

_____

20_____

_____

_____

_____

_____

20_____

_____

_____

_____

_____

20_____

_____

_____

_____

_____

20_____

_____

_____

_____

_____

"Never stop learning!" Dr. Sandra Reid

SEPTEMBER 20

20_____

_____

_____

_____

_____

20_____

_____

_____

_____

_____

20_____

_____

_____

_____

_____

20_____

_____

_____

_____

_____

20_____

_____

_____

_____

_____

SEPTEMBER 21

20_____

_____

_____

_____

_____

20_____

_____

_____

_____

_____

20_____

_____

_____

_____

_____

20_____

_____

_____

_____

_____

20_____

_____

_____

_____

_____

*"We generally change ourselves for one of two reasons:
inspiration or desperation."* Jim Rohn

SEPTEMBER 22

20_____

_____

_____

_____

_____

20_____

_____

_____

_____

_____

20_____

_____

_____

_____

_____

20_____

_____

_____

_____

_____

20_____

_____

_____

_____

_____

SEPTEMBER 23

20_____

_____

_____

_____

_____

20_____

_____

_____

_____

_____

20_____

_____

_____

_____

_____

20_____

_____

_____

_____

_____

20_____

_____

_____

_____

"The greatest danger for most of us is not that we aim too high and we miss it, but we aim too low and reach it."
Michelangelo

SEPTEMBER 24

20_____

_____
_____
_____
_____

20_____

_____
_____
_____
_____

20_____

_____
_____
_____
_____

20_____

_____
_____
_____
_____

20_____

_____
_____
_____
_____

SEPTEMBER 25

20_____

_____

_____

_____

_____

20_____

_____

_____

_____

_____

20_____

_____

_____

_____

_____

20_____

_____

_____

_____

_____

20_____

_____

_____

_____

_____

"Comfortable is the enemy of awesome."
Jennifer McClure

SEPTEMBER 26

20_____

_____

_____

_____

_____

20_____

_____

_____

_____

_____

20_____

_____

_____

_____

_____

20_____

_____

_____

_____

_____

20_____

_____

_____

_____

_____

SEPTEMBER 27

20_____

_____
_____
_____
_____

20 _____

_____
_____
_____
_____

20_____

_____
_____
_____
_____

20_____

_____
_____
_____
_____

20_____

_____
_____
_____
_____

"One man with courage makes a majority."
Andrew Jackson

SEPTEMBER 28

20_____

_____
_____
_____
_____

20_____

_____
_____
_____
_____

20_____

_____
_____
_____
_____

20_____

_____
_____
_____
_____

20_____

_____
_____
_____
_____

MILEMARKERS

SEPTEMBER 29

20_____

_____

_____

_____

_____

20_____

_____

_____

_____

_____

20_____

_____

_____

_____

_____

20_____

_____

_____

_____

_____

20_____

_____

_____

_____

_____

"The true test of a man's character is what he does when no one is watching." John Wooden

SEPTEMBER 30

20_____

_____
_____
_____
_____

20_____

_____
_____
_____
_____

20_____

_____
_____
_____
_____

20_____

_____
_____
_____
_____

20_____

_____
_____
_____
_____

MILEMARKERS

Monthly Reflections...

Favorite meal(s):

_____

_____

_____

_____

Favorite job(s):

_____

_____

_____

_____

_____

Favorite pet(s):

_____

_____

_____

_____

"The best ideas are the honest ones. Ones born out of personal experience. Ones that originated to help a few and ended up helping many." Simon Sinek

OCTOBER 1

20_____

_____
_____
_____
_____

20_____

_____
_____
_____
_____

20_____

_____
_____
_____
_____

20_____

_____
_____
_____
_____

20_____

_____
_____
_____
_____

"Don't be afraid to give up the good for the great."
John D Rockefeller

OCTOBER 2

20_____

_____

_____

_____

_____

20_____

_____

_____

_____

_____

20_____

_____

_____

_____

_____

20_____

_____

_____

_____

_____

20_____

_____

_____

_____

_____

OCTOBER 3

20_____

_____
_____
_____
_____

20_____

_____
_____
_____
_____

20_____

_____
_____
_____
_____

20_____

_____
_____
_____
_____

20_____

_____
_____
_____
_____

"Use a Career GPS (Grow Plan and Share)
for success!" Bruce Waller

OCTOBER 4

20_____

_____
_____
_____
_____

20_____

_____
_____
_____
_____

20_____

_____
_____
_____
_____

20_____

_____
_____
_____
_____

20_____

_____
_____
_____
_____

OCTOBER 5

20_____

_____
_____
_____
_____

20_____

_____
_____
_____
_____

20_____

_____
_____
_____
_____

20_____

_____
_____
_____
_____

20_____

_____
_____
_____
_____

"The people who are crazy enough to think they can change the world are the ones who do." Steve Jobs

OCTOBER 6

20_____

20_____

20_____

20_____

20_____

OCTOBER 7

20_____

_____
_____
_____
_____

20_____

_____
_____
_____
_____

20_____

_____
_____
_____
_____

20_____

_____
_____
_____
_____

20_____

_____
_____
_____
_____

_"Do what you can, with what you have,
where you are."_ Theodore Roosevelt

OCTOBER 8

20_____

_____
_____
_____
_____

20_____

_____
_____
_____
_____

20_____

_____
_____
_____
_____

20_____

_____
_____
_____
_____

20_____

_____
_____
_____
_____

OCTOBER 9

20_____

_____

_____

_____

_____

20_____

_____

_____

_____

_____

20_____

_____

_____

_____

_____

20_____

_____

_____

_____

_____

20_____

_____

_____

_____

_____

"Live simply, love generously, care deeply, speak kindly, leave the rest to God." Ronald Reagan

OCTOBER 10

20_____

_____
_____
_____
_____

20_____

_____
_____
_____
_____

20_____

_____
_____
_____
_____

20_____

_____
_____
_____
_____

20_____

_____
_____
_____
_____

OCTOBER 11

20_____

_____

_____

_____

_____

20_____

_____

_____

_____

_____

20_____

_____

_____

_____

_____

20_____

_____

_____

_____

_____

20_____

_____

_____

_____

_____

"If your actions inspire others to dream more, learn more,
do more, and become more – you are a leader."
John Quincy Adams

OCTOBER 12

20_____

_____
_____
_____
_____

20_____

_____
_____
_____
_____

20_____

_____
_____
_____
_____

20_____

_____
_____
_____
_____

20_____

_____
_____
_____
_____

OCTOBER 13

20_____

_____
_____
_____
_____

20_____

_____
_____
_____
_____

20_____

_____
_____
_____
_____

20_____

_____
_____
_____
_____

20_____

_____
_____
_____
_____

"Draw on whatever positives you can make."
Bob Stoops

OCTOBER 14

20_____

_____
_____
_____
_____

20_____

_____
_____
_____
_____

20_____

_____
_____
_____
_____

20_____

_____
_____
_____
_____

20_____

_____
_____
_____
_____

OCTOBER 15

20_____

_____

_____

_____

_____

20_____

_____

_____

_____

_____

20_____

_____

_____

_____

_____

20_____

_____

_____

_____

_____

20_____

_____

_____

_____

_____

"Every generation has a responsibility to teach the next."
Kobe Bryant

OCTOBER 16

20_____

_____
_____
_____
_____

20_____

_____
_____
_____
_____

20_____

_____
_____
_____
_____

20_____

_____
_____
_____
_____

20_____

_____
_____
_____
_____

OCTOBER 17

20_____

_____
_____
_____
_____

20_____

_____
_____
_____
_____

20_____

_____
_____
_____
_____

20_____

_____
_____
_____
_____

20_____

_____
_____
_____
_____

"You win in life with people!"
Pat Summit

OCTOBER 18

20_____

_____
_____
_____
_____

20_____

_____
_____
_____
_____

20_____

_____
_____
_____
_____

20_____

_____
_____
_____
_____

20_____

_____
_____
_____
_____

OCTOBER 19

20_____

_____
_____
_____
_____

20_____

_____
_____
_____
_____

20_____

_____
_____
_____
_____

20_____

_____
_____
_____
_____

20_____

_____
_____
_____
_____

"The one word that separates your leadership brand from others is Passion!" Mark Waller

OCTOBER 20

20_____

_____
_____
_____
_____

20_____

_____
_____
_____
_____

20_____

_____
_____
_____
_____

20_____

_____
_____
_____
_____

20_____

_____
_____
_____
_____

OCTOBER 21

20_____

_____
_____
_____
_____

20_____

_____
_____
_____
_____

20_____

_____
_____
_____
_____

20_____

_____
_____
_____
_____

20_____

_____
_____
_____
_____

"A team is not a group of people that work together.
A team is a group of people that trust each other."
Simon Sinek

OCTOBER 22

20_____

_____
_____
_____
_____

20_____

_____
_____
_____
_____

20_____

_____
_____
_____
_____

20_____

_____
_____
_____
_____

20_____

_____
_____
_____
_____

OCTOBER 23

20_____

_____
_____
_____
_____

20_____

_____
_____
_____
_____

20_____

_____
_____
_____
_____

20_____

_____
_____
_____
_____

20_____

_____
_____
_____
_____

"Be brave, be you." Yvonne K. Freeman

OCTOBER 24

20_____

_____
_____
_____
_____

20_____

_____
_____
_____
_____

20_____

_____
_____
_____
_____

20_____

_____
_____
_____
_____

20_____

_____
_____
_____
_____

OCTOBER 25

20____

20____

20____

20____

20____

"Yesterday is not ours to recover, but tomorrow is ours to win or lose." Lyndon B. Johnson

OCTOBER 26

20_____

_____

_____

_____

_____

20_____

_____

_____

_____

_____

20_____

_____

_____

_____

_____

20_____

_____

_____

_____

_____

20_____

_____

_____

_____

_____

OCTOBER 27

20_____

_____

_____

_____

_____

20_____

_____

_____

_____

_____

20_____

_____

_____

_____

_____

20_____

_____

_____

_____

_____

20_____

_____

_____

_____

_____

"What counts is not necessarily the size of the dog in the fight- it's the size of the fight in the dog."
Dwight D. Eisenhower

OCTOBER 28

20_____

_____

_____

_____

_____

20_____

_____

_____

_____

_____

20_____

_____

_____

_____

_____

20_____

_____

_____

_____

_____

20_____

_____

_____

_____

_____

OCTOBER 29

20_____

_____

_____

_____

_____

20_____

_____

_____

_____

_____

20_____

_____

_____

_____

_____

20_____

_____

_____

_____

_____

20_____

_____

_____

_____

_____

"Someday is today." Steve Gleason

OCTOBER 30

20_____

_____
_____
_____
_____

20_____

_____
_____
_____
_____

20_____

_____
_____
_____
_____

20_____

_____
_____
_____
_____

20_____

_____
_____
_____
_____

OCTOBER 31

20_____

_____

_____

_____

_____

20_____

_____

_____

_____

_____

20_____

_____

_____

_____

_____

20_____

_____

_____

_____

_____

20_____

_____

_____

_____

_____

_"Treat a man as he is, and he will remain as he is. Treat a
man as he could be, and he will become what he should be."_
Ralph Waldo Emerson

Monthly Reflections...

My favorite food/recipe to make:

_____

_____

_____

_____

_____

My favorite dessert:

_____

_____

_____

_____

My favorite holiday tradition:

_____

_____

_____

_____

"So many of our dreams seem impossible, then they seem improbable, and then, when we summon the will, they soon become inevitable." Christopher Reeve

NOVEMBER 1

20_____

_____

_____

_____

_____

20_____

_____

_____

_____

_____

20_____

_____

_____

_____

_____

20_____

_____

_____

_____

_____

20_____

_____

_____

_____

_____

"You miss 100% of the shots you don't take."
Wayne Gretzky

NOVEMBER 2

20_____

_____
_____
_____
_____

20_____

_____
_____
_____
_____

20_____

_____
_____
_____
_____

20_____

_____
_____
_____
_____

20_____

_____
_____
_____
_____

NOVEMBER 3

20_____

_____
_____
_____
_____

20_____

_____
_____
_____
_____

20_____

_____
_____
_____
_____

20_____

_____
_____
_____
_____

20_____

_____
_____
_____
_____

"Do your best and don't let someone else set your standards." Bill Russell

NOVEMBER 4

20_____

_____
_____
_____
_____

20_____

_____
_____
_____
_____

20_____

_____
_____
_____
_____

20_____

_____
_____
_____
_____

20_____

_____
_____
_____
_____

NOVEMBER 5

20_____

_____

_____

_____

_____

20_____

_____

_____

_____

_____

20_____

_____

_____

_____

_____

20_____

_____

_____

_____

_____

20_____

_____

_____

_____

_____

*"Volunteering is a great way to grow your leadership
while serving the community. Get Involved!"*
Bruce Waller

NOVEMBER 6

20____

_____
_____
_____
_____

20____

_____
_____
_____
_____

20____

_____
_____
_____
_____

20____

_____
_____
_____
_____

20____

_____
_____
_____
_____

NOVEMBER 7

20_____

_____

_____

_____

_____

20_____

_____

_____

_____

_____

20_____

_____

_____

_____

_____

20_____

_____

_____

_____

_____

20_____

_____

_____

_____

_____

"He learned, he loved, he became better."
Mitch Albom

NOVEMBER 8

20_____

_____

_____

_____

_____

20_____

_____

_____

_____

_____

20_____

_____

_____

_____

_____

20_____

_____

_____

_____

_____

20_____

_____

_____

_____

_____

NOVEMBER 9

20_____

_____
_____
_____
_____

20_____

_____
_____
_____
_____

20_____

_____
_____
_____
_____

20_____

_____
_____
_____
_____

20_____

_____
_____
_____
_____

"One of the best reasons for keeping quiet is it can't be repeated to anyone." Lillian V. Fults

NOVEMBER 10

20_____

_____
_____
_____
_____

20_____

_____
_____
_____
_____

20_____

_____
_____
_____
_____

20_____

_____
_____
_____
_____

20_____

_____
_____
_____
_____

NOVEMBER 11

20_____

_____

_____

_____

_____

20_____

_____

_____

_____

_____

20_____

_____

_____

_____

_____

20_____

_____

_____

_____

_____

20_____

_____

_____

_____

_____

"Ask yourself… What do I need to start doing, stop doing, or continue doing for success?" Dale Carnegie

NOVEMBER 12

20_____

_____
_____
_____
_____

20_____

_____
_____
_____
_____

20_____

_____
_____
_____
_____

20_____

_____
_____
_____
_____

20_____

_____
_____
_____
_____

NOVEMBER 13

20_____

_____

_____

_____

20_____

_____

_____

_____

20_____

_____

_____

_____

20_____

_____

_____

_____

20_____

_____

_____

_____

"Motivation is what gets you started. Habits is what keeps you going." Jim Rohn

NOVEMBER 14

20_____

_____
_____
_____
_____

20_____

_____
_____
_____
_____

20_____

_____
_____
_____
_____

20_____

_____
_____
_____
_____

20_____

_____
_____
_____
_____

NOVEMBER 15

20_____

_____

_____

_____

_____

20_____

_____

_____

_____

_____

20_____

_____

_____

_____

_____

20_____

_____

_____

_____

_____

20_____

_____

_____

_____

_____

"Fear freezes us. Being bold frees us!" Peggy Smith

NOVEMBER 16

20_____

_____

_____

_____

_____

20_____

_____

_____

_____

_____

20_____

_____

_____

_____

_____

20_____

_____

_____

_____

_____

20_____

_____

_____

_____

_____

NOVEMBER 17

20_____

_____
_____
_____
_____

20_____

_____
_____
_____
_____

20_____

_____
_____
_____
_____

20_____

_____
_____
_____
_____

20_____

_____
_____
_____
_____

"Leadership is someone who brings people together."
George W. Bush

NOVEMBER 18

20_____

_____
_____
_____
_____

20_____

_____
_____
_____
_____

20_____

_____
_____
_____
_____

20_____

_____
_____
_____
_____

20_____

_____
_____
_____
_____

NOVEMBER 19

20_____

_____
_____
_____
_____

20_____

_____
_____
_____
_____

20_____

_____
_____
_____
_____

20_____

_____
_____
_____
_____

20_____

_____
_____
_____
_____

"If you just work for the money, you'll never make it, but if you love what you're doing and always put the customer first, success will be yours." Ray Kroc

NOVEMBER 20

20_____

_____
_____
_____
_____

20_____

_____
_____
_____
_____

20_____

_____
_____
_____
_____

20_____

_____
_____
_____
_____

20_____

_____
_____
_____
_____

NOVEMBER 21

20_____

_____
_____
_____
_____

20_____

_____
_____
_____
_____

20_____

_____
_____
_____
_____

20_____

_____
_____
_____
_____

20_____

_____
_____
_____
_____

"There are three types of people in this world, those that make it happen, those who watch it happen, and those who wonder what happened." Mary Kay Ash

NOVEMBER 22

20_____

_____
_____
_____
_____

20_____

_____
_____
_____
_____

20_____

_____
_____
_____
_____

20_____

_____
_____
_____
_____

20_____

_____
_____
_____
_____

NOVEMBER 23

20_____

_____
_____
_____
_____

20_____

_____
_____
_____
_____

20_____

_____
_____
_____
_____

20_____

_____
_____
_____
_____

20_____

_____
_____
_____
_____

"No trend goes on forever." Lee J. Colan

NOVEMBER 24

20_____

_____

_____

_____

_____

20_____

_____

_____

_____

_____

20_____

_____

_____

_____

_____

20_____

_____

_____

_____

_____

20_____

_____

_____

_____

_____

NOVEMBER 25

20_____

_____

_____

_____

_____

20_____

_____

_____

_____

_____

20_____

_____

_____

_____

_____

20_____

_____

_____

_____

_____

20_____

_____

_____

_____

_____

"The object of love is to serve, not to win."
Woodrow Wilson

NOVEMBER 26

20_____

_____
_____
_____
_____

20_____

_____
_____
_____
_____

20_____

_____
_____
_____
_____

20_____

_____
_____
_____
_____

20_____

_____
_____
_____
_____

MILEMARKERS

NOVEMBER 27

20_____

_____
_____
_____
_____

20_____

_____
_____
_____
_____

20_____

_____
_____
_____
_____

20_____

_____
_____
_____
_____

20_____

_____
_____
_____
_____

"One life can, and always does, change the world."
John O'Leary

NOVEMBER 28

20_____

_____
_____
_____
_____

20_____

_____
_____
_____
_____

20_____

_____
_____
_____
_____

20_____

_____
_____
_____
_____

20_____

_____
_____
_____
_____

NOVEMBER 29

20_____

_____
_____
_____
_____

20_____

_____
_____
_____
_____

20_____

_____
_____
_____
_____

20_____

_____
_____
_____
_____

20_____

_____
_____
_____
_____

"In the world of business, the people who are most successful are those who are doing what they love."
Warren Buffet

NOVEMBER 30

20_____

_____
_____
_____
_____

20_____

_____
_____
_____
_____

20_____

_____
_____
_____
_____

20_____

_____
_____
_____
_____

20_____

_____
_____
_____
_____

Monthly Reflections...

How many times have I relocated and from/to where?

_____

_____

_____

_____

_____

My favorite house/city to live in:

_____

_____

_____

My most prized collection at home is:

_____

_____

_____

"Once you've established the goals you want and the price you're willing to pay, you can ignore the minor hurts, the opponent's pressure, and the temporary setbacks." Vince Lombardi

DECEMBER 1

20_____

_____
_____
_____
_____

20_____

_____
_____
_____
_____

20_____

_____
_____
_____
_____

20_____

_____
_____
_____
_____

20_____

_____
_____
_____
_____

"A gambler's money has no home." Dewey Ivey

DECEMBER 2

20_____

_____

_____

_____

_____

20_____

_____

_____

_____

_____

20_____

_____

_____

_____

_____

20_____

_____

_____

_____

_____

20_____

_____

_____

_____

_____

DECEMBER 3

20_____

_____
_____
_____
_____

20_____

_____
_____
_____
_____

20_____

_____
_____
_____
_____

20_____

_____
_____
_____
_____

20_____

_____
_____
_____
_____

"Excellence is on the other side of obstacles." Greg Hawks

DECEMBER 4

20_____

_____
_____
_____
_____

20_____

_____
_____
_____
_____

20_____

_____
_____
_____
_____

20_____

_____
_____
_____
_____

20_____

_____
_____
_____
_____

DECEMBER 5

20_____

_____

_____

_____

_____

20_____

_____

_____

_____

_____

20_____

_____

_____

_____

_____

20_____

_____

_____

_____

_____

20_____

_____

_____

_____

_____

"Don't worry until you have something to worry about." Martha Ellen Causey Thornton

DECEMBER 6

20_____

_____
_____
_____
_____

20_____

_____
_____
_____
_____

20_____

_____
_____
_____
_____

20_____

_____
_____
_____
_____

20_____

_____
_____
_____
_____

DECEMBER 7

20_____

_____
_____
_____
_____

20_____

_____
_____
_____
_____

20_____

_____
_____
_____
_____

20_____

_____
_____
_____
_____

20_____

_____
_____
_____
_____

"My job is to know what creates value."
Caroline Carter

DECEMBER 8

20_____

_____
_____
_____
_____

20_____

_____
_____
_____
_____

20_____

_____
_____
_____
_____

20_____

_____
_____
_____
_____

20_____

_____
_____
_____
_____

DECEMBER 9

20_____

_____
_____
_____
_____

20_____

_____
_____
_____
_____

20_____

_____
_____
_____
_____

20_____

_____
_____
_____
_____

20_____

_____
_____
_____
_____

"Good times never felt so good!" Lionel Richie

DECEMBER 10

20_____

_____
_____
_____
_____

20_____

_____
_____
_____
_____

20_____

_____
_____
_____
_____

20_____

_____
_____
_____
_____

20_____

_____
_____
_____
_____

DECEMBER 11

20_____

_____

_____

_____

_____

20_____

_____

_____

_____

_____

20_____

_____

_____

_____

_____

20_____

_____

_____

_____

_____

20_____

_____

_____

_____

_____

"Find Your Lane and Accelerate Your Career!"
Bruce Waller

DECEMBER 12

20_____

_____
_____
_____
_____

20_____

_____
_____
_____
_____

20_____

_____
_____
_____
_____

20_____

_____
_____
_____
_____

20_____

_____
_____
_____
_____

DECEMBER 13

20_____

_____

_____

_____

_____

20_____

_____

_____

_____

_____

20_____

_____

_____

_____

_____

20_____

_____

_____

_____

_____

20_____

_____

_____

_____

_____

"To have more, we must become more." Jim Rohn

DECEMBER 14

20_____

_____
_____
_____
_____

20_____

_____
_____
_____
_____

20_____

_____
_____
_____
_____

20_____

_____
_____
_____
_____

20_____

_____
_____
_____
_____

DECEMBER 15

20_____

_____

_____

_____

_____

20_____

_____

_____

_____

_____

20_____

_____

_____

_____

_____

20_____

_____

_____

_____

_____

20_____

_____

_____

_____

_____

"Sometimes bringing value can be as simple as showing up with a smile." Bruce Waller

DECEMBER 16

20_____

_____

_____

_____

_____

20_____

_____

_____

_____

_____

20_____

_____

_____

_____

_____

20_____

_____

_____

_____

_____

20_____

_____

_____

_____

_____

DECEMBER 17

20_____

_____
_____
_____
_____

20_____

_____
_____
_____
_____

20_____

_____
_____
_____
_____

20_____

_____
_____
_____
_____

20_____

_____
_____
_____
_____

"Be the change that you wish to see in the world."
Mahatma Gandhi

DECEMBER 18

20____

_____
_____
_____
_____

20____

_____
_____
_____
_____

20____

_____
_____
_____
_____

20____

_____
_____
_____
_____

20____

_____
_____
_____
_____

MILEMARKERS

DECEMBER 19

20_____

_____
_____
_____
_____

20_____

_____
_____
_____
_____

20_____

_____
_____
_____
_____

20_____

_____
_____
_____
_____

20_____

_____
_____
_____
_____

"Do you know what my favorite part of the game is?
The opportunity to play." Mike Singletary

DECEMBER 20

20_____

_____

_____

_____

_____

20_____

_____

_____

_____

_____

20_____

_____

_____

_____

_____

20_____

_____

_____

_____

_____

20_____

_____

_____

_____

_____

DECEMBER 21

20_____

_____

_____

_____

_____

20_____

_____

_____

_____

_____

20_____

_____

_____

_____

_____

20_____

_____

_____

_____

_____

20_____

_____

_____

_____

_____

"It's easier to say yes to a plan than an idea."
Dr. Daren Martin

DECEMBER 22

20_____

_____
_____
_____
_____

20_____

_____
_____
_____
_____

20_____

_____
_____
_____
_____

20_____

_____
_____
_____
_____

20_____

_____
_____
_____
_____

DECEMBER 23

20_____

_____
_____
_____
_____

20_____

_____
_____
_____
_____

20_____

_____
_____
_____
_____

20_____

_____
_____
_____
_____

20_____

_____
_____
_____
_____

"It's no biggie." Martha Ellen Causey Thornton

DECEMBER 24

20____

_____
_____
_____
_____

20____

_____
_____
_____
_____

20____

_____
_____
_____
_____

20____

_____
_____
_____
_____

20____

_____
_____
_____
_____

MILEMARKERS

DECEMBER 25

20_____

_____
_____
_____
_____

20_____

_____
_____
_____
_____

20_____

_____
_____
_____
_____

20_____

_____
_____
_____
_____

20_____

_____
_____
_____
_____

"No man is a failure who has friends."
Clarence

DECEMBER 26

20_____

_____
_____
_____
_____

20_____

_____
_____
_____
_____

20_____

_____
_____
_____
_____

20_____

_____
_____
_____
_____

20_____

_____
_____
_____
_____

DECEMBER 27

20_____

_____

_____

_____

_____

20_____

_____

_____

_____

_____

20_____

_____

_____

_____

_____

20_____

_____

_____

_____

_____

20_____

_____

_____

_____

_____

"Always be yourself unless you can be a unicorn, then always be a unicorn." Tim Sackett

DECEMBER 28

20_____

_____
_____
_____
_____

20_____

_____
_____
_____
_____

20_____

_____
_____
_____
_____

20_____

_____
_____
_____
_____

20_____

_____
_____
_____
_____

DECEMBER 29

20_____

_____
_____
_____
_____

20_____

_____
_____
_____
_____

20_____

_____
_____
_____
_____

20_____

_____
_____
_____
_____

20_____

_____
_____
_____
_____

"Oh God, thy sea is so great and my boat is so small."
John F. Kennedy

DECEMBER 30

20_____

_____
_____
_____
_____

20_____

_____
_____
_____
_____

20_____

_____
_____
_____
_____

20_____

_____
_____
_____
_____

20_____

_____
_____
_____
_____

DECEMBER 31

20_____

_____
_____
_____
_____

20_____

_____
_____
_____
_____

20_____

_____
_____
_____
_____

20_____

_____
_____
_____
_____

20_____

_____
_____
_____
_____

"All of our dreams can come true, if we have the courage to pursue them." Walt Disney